KATABATIC CIRCUS

VOLUME 1

AN ANTHOLOGY OF SPECULATIVE POETICS

Edited by
NAOMI SIMONE BORWEIN

To the speculative reality of fabulist life...

CONTENTS

FOREWORD

Welcome to the circus. I will be your ringmaster.

This is the inaugural issue of *Katabatic Circus* (Volume 1), an annual poetry anthology that showcases literary speculative poetry. In this textual hinterland, we find the genrefication of theoretical and practical poetics.

The aesthetic approach of the anthology draws on the complex metaphor of the **katabatic imagination** (as the hero's sojourn down into the underworld) and the geomorphic power of katabatic arctic winds (as a yawing between material states and realities). It is this dynamic nexus of meaning-materiality that is intended; the pieces in this volume are complex, nuanced, thought-provoking works that manifest such an ontological and phenomenological space. But in this space, pieces invoke slipstream, fabulist, and magical realist aesthetics, as well as multivalent, metaverse, and meta-modernist approaches and theoretics.

Contributors to the *Katabatic Circus* experientially employ various poetry styles from ersatz found poetry to imagism. From the slipstream, mixed media, experimental style of Pixie Bruner to the visual poetry of K. Albasi, pieces actively adapt traditional poetry forms.

Stephanie M. Wytovich's "On the Edge of Worlds" is a rich reinterpretation of the poetic veil between the living and the dead. Geneve Flynn's pantoum poem, "how to write an elegy," draws the reader down through quatrains of complex grief. Ambrose West offers an speculative evocation of trans identity. Özge Lena's linguistic Big Top in "Dark Horse of My Childhood" and "Abandoned Circus" are etched in a haunting, dark confessional style. Dianthe West wields a beautiful symbolic and mythic array in "Gorgoneion." In this volume, you will find the organic decay of H.V. Patterson's "God is Now the Machine" or the Shirley Jackson-inspired horror of "Whatever Walked There Walked Alone." In "The Silver Tree" and "Bloody Thursday," the horror realism of Alan Magee's historio-cultural, literary lens is palpable.

I invite you to consume these pieces in the spirit with which they were meant to be consumed.

Enjoy the show.

—Naomi Simone Borwein,
November 2024

ON THE EDGE OF WORLDS

STEPHANIE M. WYTOVICH

Honeycomb and pomegranate seeds, you search under
worlds for split tongues / open doors. The spider webs
in your eyes a veil between death and the dead / descending
into catacombs There are whispers in those bones, songs
in the three frozen heads of dogs. Their teeth in your palms /
bleeding secrets like sap.

You rise from ice, a spirit / trumpet dripping
the forgotten words of seances. This asphodel garden /
bedding for planchette scars, the coffin blanket
covering your grave. Stitch up your stigmata / bind your feet
with black glass. You walked with monsters
now the hanged man must scream:
Heaven a figment, a ghastly mirage—

      cut your loss against the scales of sirens /
      kiss the womb of Scylla as you drown.

HOW TO WRITE AN ELEGY

GENEVE FLYNN

how to write an elegy:
cancelled appointments. falter.
ghost/scent your echo is here
but I don't remember you

cancelled appointments. falter.
new pieces piecemeal appear
but I don't remember you
old fragments collate depart

new piecemeal pieces appear
tack together best I can
old fragments depart collate
who you were and where you are

tack together best I can
travel gear/spirit money
where you are and who you were
buys entry down to Diyu

travel gear/spirit money

thin underworld currency
buys entry down to Diyu—
not news of your arrival

thin underworld currency
tumbles down ten courts of hell
no news of your arrival
to stop my descent. I fall

tumble down ten courts of hell
weighted by crimes I forget
to stop my descent. I fall
Goddess of Oblivion

weighed for my crimes, to forget
I am aided by Meng Po
Goddess of Oblivion
bittersweet rebirth wiped clear

I am aided by Meng Po
without a thing to hold to
bittersweet rebirth wipes clean
who I was and who I am

without a thing to hold to
I can no longer compose
who I am and who I was
since cancellations. falter.

I can no longer compose
myself to write an elegy
since cancellations. falter.
ghost/scent your echo is here

Diyu: the realm of the dead in Chinese mythology. All souls go to the underworld after death and pass through the ten courts of hell, where physical punishment is meted out for earthly crimes.

Spirit money: a form of joss paper used in Chinese ancestral worship. The paper is burned to provide for the deceased in the afterlife.

Meng Po: the Goddess of Forgetfulness. Once a soul passes through all ten levels of hell, she offers a draught to wipe away memories of past lives and torments, preparing a clean slate for reincarnation.

This poem explores the confusion and sense of freefall I experienced after the recent death of my father, whom I thought I knew but hardly knew at all, and my efforts to trace who he was.

ROADSIDE SOUVENIRS; OR, THE GENREFICATION OF FEMICIDE IN SERIAL KILLER TALES

NAOMI SIMONE BORWEIN

There is a rest stop in Upstate New York.
You will know it when you feel it.
Like the slave quarters at the old sugar plantation
    outside of Lake Jackson,
the earth leeches echoes
of where the stygian river once raged with their
    blood.

You climb a beautiful hill, framed by atmospheric
    blue, lens flares;
it rises into a vertical skyline of cirrus wisps,
fractostratus, and cumulus clouds,
almost invisible as you enter twilight.

There is a little tarmac road that leads to a restroom
    next to a lamppost.
The lights flickering, bugs drawn to the electric heat
    of the bulb,
and an 'uncanny' silence.
Spreading.
Deadening.

Not even the insects *daring to speak.*

You enter the restroom.
A small brick house, a row of stalls,
with every step a sense of unease builds.

At the far end of the restroom,
you paint a picture.
Flash filled with a woman,
spread-eagled and drained of blood in the back stall.
Look up, and see a small window she is dragged
    through.

You convince yourself,
certain it was a serial killer's old haunt.

Was it Bundy?
the Son of Sam?
or the BTK killer taking a road trip?

Someone unknown?

You flee.
Heart pounding,
looking back over your shoulder as you drive.
The shadows of trees caving in behind—
suberin-bone digits grasping at, as you escape.

Later you start imagining dead women
everywhere.
Trophies become roadkill.
Roadkill becomes human beings' haphazard forms.
Cold case obsession takes hold.

You are driving up through The Natchez Trace.
There is a
sudden onslaught of sirens,

federal patrol vehicles
doing U-turns,
a giant semi cork screwed into the median
with a tiny blue Reno, [pranged] steel accordion
    behind it,

the body of a woman
pinned to her steering wheel like an insect to a
    board,
limbs limp, head drooping forward.

They weave in and out of traffic,
a stretch of highway burying
the sedan that caused it.

Ten years before,
a sandy-haired teenage girl jaywalking—crossing
    before an intersection
off Honeysuckle,
T-boned at 60 miles an hour by a large white van,
    accelerating,
she sails through the air
gracefully,
dead *before* she hits the concrete;
the van speeds on not even pausing to look back.
You imagine a calling card
pinwheeling off her corpse
in an exaggerated parabola.

In the early summer,
at rush hour on Wonderland Road,
a blond college girl
entangled with her bike.
Head gashed open
blood coating her hands, chin, eyes,
and the look of *horror* on her stained face.
People are mesmerized.

Then on August fourth,
the limp body of a teenage girl
in jean shorts.
Her purse strewn across the road.
Two men lift her from a lane of traffic.
And set her down on the verge.
They shake her body,
her feet turning inwards,
at unnatural angles,
until *it* looks like a reanimated corpse seizing.
A grotesque man in a green shirt stands on the side-
    line, filming the spectacle.
Two women with *horror*-struck faces unable to look
    away.

You are shunted onto another road,
and when you circle back
her body is gone.

The scene
obscured by vehicles
sagging feet
the tendons in her thighs, faceless.

You never do find out what really happened.

ACROSS THE WAY

KURT NEWTON

Across the way,
she would always go,
when times were sad,
or simply too much
for her head to handle.

Across the road,
into the woods,
where sunlight streamed
like a great golden gown
draped across the wild.

Along the way,
she met silver birch
shag bark hickory,
oak and ash and toadstools
by the dozen.

Along the path,
her feet walked upon
the soft grass of spring,

the creeping vines of summer,
the crisp leaves of autumn.

Along the way,
she would sit and rest,
collect her thoughts,
forget about the loneliness
that waited for her back home.

But over time,
the years wore her down,
her ailing mother died,
leaving her with an empty house,
an empty life.

Across the way,
she found herself
more often than not,
at home among the leaves,
the trees and woodland flowers.

And one day,
when she decided to sit
and not get up,
there came a rustling in the woods,
and the little people came out.

They were the children
she never had,
grandkids and family friends,
they surrounded her like saplings
surround a mother tree.

It was the time of her life,
a whirlwind of endless talk
and catching up,
and laughter till the sun

finally set.

After many days,
and weeks and months,
she became the soft grass of spring,
the creeping vines of summer,
the crisp leaves of autumn.

Across the way,
new people now own the house,
a lonely girl,
much like herself,
ventures into the woods.

SUNSET CIRCLE

KURT NEWTON

where farmland ends
in a cul-de-sac
where homes rise
like monoliths
to catch the evening colors
where fat cows lounge
wine in hand
scotch on the rocks
basking on backyard patios
steaks sizzling in the dusk
where night falls
like junk stock sell-offs
where sticks snap
at the edge of the woods
and shadows hug the ground
like black clouds moving
across an inverted sky
where security codes
trigger motion sensors
splashing white light
upon the darkness

like a bucket of paint thrown
on a priceless masterpiece
where bathrobes and lingerie
appear in doorways
some with handguns
gripped in cloven hooves
where insects pause
and shadows pool
and all is still
but the waiting

WE ALL WENT TO THE RIVER

KURT NEWTON

We all went to the river
to drown ourselves
in its mighty depths.
We stood on the banks
and one by one
we ambled in.
The river took us
by the ankles,
then by the legs,
until we were waist-deep,
our gowns billowing beside us
like blanched lily pads.
At last, the water
grabbed us by the neck
and pushed us under,
once, twice, three times
into its bosom,
making sure we tasted
its cool devouring nature.
And then it released us
to float downstream,

like pale boats
seeking that speck of land
that called to us the loudest.
We washed ashore,
our bodies rich with purpose,
fingers grasping,
gripping the land,
our feet once again
sinking into the soil.

THE TIDAL BASIN

KURT NEWTON

They say the sea
once rose here,
an ebb and flow
as high as a two-story building,
like the breathing of a great beast
on the ocean floor.
But when the developers came,
in their three-piece suits
and offshore bank accounts,
they saw an opportunity,
and they took it.

Fishermen abandoned their slips
and moved up the coast.
The village that once harbored
tackle shops and engine repair,
and breakfast as greasy as
as a freshly-netted cod—
a community—was sold.
The tide was gated, diverted.
Boutiques and office space,

cafes, delis and B&Bs.
The village was now upscale.
The great beast held its breath,
and, one night, let it out slowly.

A pale blue mist lined the tidal basin
and crawled ashore, ankle deep
Some thought nothing of it,
believing it to be an annual event
brought on by a seasonal algae
or a particular phase of the moon.
Party-goers danced in the streets,
tumblers in hand,
as the blue tide moved about their ankles
like dry ice on a concert stage.

But the mist kept rising,
the pale blue filling the canal-like streets,
the shops and restaurants mimicking the steep walls
of a glacial fjord.
Some began to see ghosts in the unusual fog,
glimpses of drunken fishermen
from an era gone by.
And there were other apparitions,
shark-like beasts with long snouts
and even longer teeth
swimming through the intersections.

Soon the mist had risen
as high as a two-story building,
and those asleep in their memory foam beds
began to dream of monstrous things from the deep
too hideous to describe
and too frightening to ever forget.
Eventually, the phenomenon subsided,
the blue mist returning to the sea,
and the village awoke the next morning

changed.

Visitors left and never came back.
Travelers seeking rest and relaxation
found only unease.
Retailers and restaurateurs
gradually abandoned ship.
For Sale signs were as common as the seagulls.
The village had lost its allure,
beginning with that night
when the blue mist rose up like a tide
and the basin's true identity was revealed.

The bait shops and engine repair have since returned.
Fisherman now dock in the bay.
The tidal gates have been disabled
and the people of the village welcome
the rise and fall
and all that comes with it,
the squirming, swimming, teeming life
that breaks the surface,
and the memories that lie silent
at the bottom.

GENITIVE CARNIS

KATHLEEN HELLEN

On the blue velvet couch, beside where they'd hung *Christ in Gethsemane*, where I'd curled up like a slug to watch the vampire on tv, I slipped the pretty buttons on my flannel, shoved my hand into my pants—what I wanted more than wings was to be the wife of the Eternal. Not the bride, veiled, in white, clutching rosaries and white carnations. I wanted two red buds sprouting from my neck, two punctures in the flesh to prove the pleasure.

I turned my head and what slipped in? A mirror, my face a strange bouquet before the bloom went fetid.

GORGONEION

DIANTHE WEST

I came upon a creature in the bath,
her mosaic gaze bent by the hot emerald water—
with curled gold-strand tresses waving like autumn
    kelp;
I dreamt one day I'd turn a fluid key
and release her.

Her silken hair flowed through my bare legs,
mingled with mine like funerary threads.
Blood, heat hung in the gravely mist,
green veins swirling with golden silt.

And so it went,
until the day she pulled me under.
I plunged through the vaults of the cloaca,
past gems from fine rings,
ossified persons,
shards of amphorae,
and down to the sea.
There, Stheno, Euryale emerged from bronze
    shipwrecks;

wailing like flutes, they offered me a cup.

I drank the sweet blood of the giant;
grasped the feather of the white horse.
My hair spun wildly about my head,
coiled, hissing, full of life.

In the brutalized body of their sister,
my thick eel-like body slithers out from the water.
My whip tail sways—
red upon red walls,
fractured in the steam drains with blood, bone, and
    flesh.

DARK HORSE OF MY CHILDHOOD

ÖZGE LENA

Tell me I have nothing
to despair, nothing to fear,
the dark horse is not real,

it is not hungry, not craving
for my body. Tell me I do
not need to feed it with tears,

alcohol, semen. Poor animals
dying inside me are just thirsty.
Tell me this is not an actual fall

like the one that crumbled me
when I was sent to a boarding
school to learn how to ride all

alone for the rest of my life,
how to look the horse right
in the eye, its toothed wells.

After my childhood—an empty
carousel in an abandoned circus,
whirling in vain, in vain, in vain.

ABANDONED CIRCUS

ÖZGE LENA

An acid coloured abandoned city
left behind by climate nomads
with a ruinous circus in it.

The air smells of rust and rue.
A tiger roars.

The stage of the abandoned circus
left behind by a clamorous crowd
at a stroke in a frisson of fear.

The air smells of wine and woe.
A leopard roars.

On the abandoned stage lies a fallen
C next to an enormous doll stuffed with
the remains of heat-stricken humans.

The air smells of cinder and anger.
A jaguar roars.

Then a festive jukebox vomits coins right
before it starts to play a joyful song
of green times before the wildfires.
The doll chuckles with a hyena
laugh. The song deadens. I
falls on the doll's head.
R swings in silence.

On the wall neon letters smell of dark desires.
A panther roars.

All of a sudden a thunder. C. A lightning swords
the clouds of cirrus. U. Over the circus
collapses venomous weather. S.

The air smells of a merry apocalypse.

KATABATIC CIRCUS

HOW TO EXIT A VEHICLE LIKE A DIGNIFIED WOMAN

CHARLOTTE COSGROVE

I try to cross my legs the way you taught me
And swear less in the company of others.

When exiting a vehicle keep your knees together
Twist your body clockwise.
Twirl from the footwell—
Dignified and worthy
A ballerina of the mundane.

When talking to others do not use rude language.
Nobody likes a potty mouth.

How unfortunate as I keep my legs together
And my lady parts sufficiently hidden—
I fall, an unbalanced worm
Corkscrewing to the ground.
Profanity jumps from my mouth
...
For fuck's sake.

And it twists to shape your perception—
And, regrettably, my undergarments are visible.

X. LA ROUE DE FORTUNE— REVERSED

TRIPP J CROUSE

Your body, a blank asphalt canvas,
tagged with various graffitied phrases,
a sharp voice, gravity and grit,
the slightest echo of disdain,
like tattooed skin on an apparition.

As a dead man, I do not submit
to your notions of honor[*]—
our past is but ripples
in an ever-flowing stream
toward a neon god.[†]

But if I were a ghost
permitted to say goodbye
before I died,
I would haunt your mountains,

---

[*] Paraphrase from Ridley Scott, "The Duelists" (film, 1977)
[†] Inspired by Simon & Garfunkel, "The Sound of Silence" (1964)

trees, and empty rooms, forever,
to remind you
that you
were someone's dream once.

nsb

IN WHICH I TELL YOU SPECULATIVE FICTION IS THE TRANS BODY

WEST AMBROSE

speculated upon by cis and by trans, speculated by his and hers
and theirs, too. speculated in magazines and speculated across
dinner tables (*the white, no, the red, thank you—*) speculated in

pristine classrooms and the seedy corners of queer clubs
(*What's in your, ah nevermind–*) at bus stops and bathhouses
and bedrooms where shutters cannot cast out the panopticon
of horror after horror after horror; your body is a vampire

and your body is a lament, your body is a funeral that
walks and talks and breathes fearfully, your body is
a corpse before it knows how to die; half-alive, waiting
to be the (over)medicalized slab on Frankenstein's

gurney, speculated on whether: *Surgery is killing you*

or *Feeding what kills you.* leeches. locked-rooms.

lachrymose banshees shrieking *Are you too close-minded*

to still wear a dress? Regardless, are you too narrow-minded

to be feminine, go on be feminine, we will never, ever love

you unless you're good and docile and feminine–

Waiting to be the ghost who overhears the wrong

pronouns: *What were they* and *Who were they,*

and *Funny how you learn the word 'they' when*

you're too afraid to say Him; speculation of friends

and families and lovers who ask if you're on T as if

 it's a rite of passage, then growl at your voice as if

it's a petal to be torn, never a wish to be granted;

what if that's just how it is?

Anger upon Anger upon Anger speculates, feeding on another,

so many teeth into one little body... In the night, I wonder

Does speculation even continue in Death? I light the votive

of my chest and let it burn down past my thighs. In the circle

of someone else's wishes, chalk-kissed and

blood-flushed, I find a man who has so many names,

we forget to exchange them; first the glances, hard and hotly,

next the touches bold as Despair, his rough thatch against my

calla lily, his tender flood against my ravine; over and under,

plunging with thunder, the harpsichord strikes for each lonely

soul on this planet; his mouth on my Divinity, my tongue at

his Antiquity, his violin strung taut across the bedpost of

my wrists; the harpoon, the harbinger, the omen, the calyx;

the cusp of a prayer to the god of his heartbeat; the hailstorm,

the horsemen, the heavens that never will hear, the glint of

what my iridescent choir-boy throat sings—

In the dark, he trembles next to me, imperfect rib

to rib; his whispers buried in my sternum;

Do you think anyone still remembers

to draw my wings?

WHAT WE HEARD IN THE PERIODICALS SECTIONS (1861-1893)

WEST AMBROSE

Have you ever tasted it?

        And would you know what it takes to

make it sting?

     The whispers light as doves, through the stacks, flourishing.

Their

  feathers fall

     on your face, brush the curious

whim

      of such a wandering ear; *Do you know how you'd*

        like to— I mean, now, and even here

           with your Thirst

             still unnamed,

        Do you want me to show you

     how to change?

The index of pearl-white pages slowly decaying, tanned and hardened
edges, pressed back to back, produces such a myriad of sounds;

rustle, brush, reiterate

       the strike of

           leatheredspinetoleatheredspine

; the precise absence

       of breath

         Drenched

          with meaning;

             the petal-flames of rain,

                 pooling

waxen

    downpour

       to blindfold yourself by; the aurora of a bite,

              the bite of silk,

slipping; *drink of my body and I'll drink of yours,*

           we'll cease to be as we were;

we'll never sleep again...

      slipping haunt after haunt,

    the fore edge

        clenched between

           incisors, grinding down

to hone these exquisite pains;

     the other men

will all grow old one day—

> *we'll be growing out our fangs.*

URSILLO

WEST AMBROSE

At the edge of the slate-soaked town,

where once each man came to drown,

was now the shell of a tiny crown,

made from the washed-up and watered down—

Each evening farmers sold their wares,

and the city-dwellers perfected stares,

through the fog-leeching mist,

to scare even the most jovial tourist.

Night passed into night and old myths withered,

on tongues too ashamed to speak of bitter

freedom wrung from the mistakes,

lack of agency— Society so often breaks

. . .

forth and buries our desires out of fear:

someone will see you, someone will hear

that your heart is different and your body is too—

(there's no proper way to exist, if that person is You.)

There, on the edge of the cliffs lived a young man,

Ursillo, with hair the colour of wheat and a painter's tan;

each afternoon he took to his perch and waited

for sunset, dusk-rise, midnight to be elated.

He created the marvel of each sky before him.

There was no greater joy than his painter's whim,

shading and mixing and tainting,

each blue into lilac, each buttercup into lightning.

Often, his afternoons slipped quick into evenings.

Too late, he packed up his canvas and brushes, heaving—

Too late, he walked alone along the shoreline and bushes,

save for the warning of nest-huddled swallows and thrushes.

One night, a figure slithered forth from the rustling dark,

fangs sharp, with scale-clad hands that reached stark

into the midst of the Night, and pulled at his waist,

before exclaiming in alarm 'Sorry sir, I couldn't quite see your face!'

. . .

The creature stepped forward, slipping into the light,

he looked to be a few years younger than Ursillo might—

he was lithe and dark-haired, with a terrible grin,

and the softest brown eyes Ursillo had ever witnessed.

'Who are you?' he asked, after he let out a scream of woe.

'I'm John. And You must be Ursillo.'

How do you know me? He wanted to say, words water-logged in his mind.

'You are Ursillo. Sir, *you* are one of my kind.'

Your kind...? Ursillo drew back from the fair boy,

then readied his brushes like a navy-branded toy;

bayonets or ship artillery for battle,

and felt something in his queer chest rattle:

How could the strange boy see, even in this dark

his hands, webbed at birth, had formed the mark

of horned and scaled features, where should be

proper, working hands—how *could* he see?

Was he like the rest in such a narrow coastal town?

Would he try to snap his brushes and throw his easel down?

Instead, the boy smiled, picked up what he dropped,

and sat down beside him– then, the whole world stopped.

. . .

'You are Ursillo, you are one of my kind. A dying kind.'

'Oh.' He replied. 'I... didn't pay such rumors any mind.'

'Your mother was very unhappy. And not a good person at all.'

'No, Nor am I. In a much different way, if you recall

humans are loathsome to what they don't understand, other creatures—'

'I can't quite say I do.' An innocent look crossed his young features.

'Let's just say, if they saw the scales upon your skin,

and... the tail? Well, *their* patience would wear thin.'

'Why would anyone wear a patience so, so... thin?'

'Translation: they would kill you–- then, kill you again.'

'I don't believe you!' John cried. 'Please, take me to see your town.

It looks so beautiful from the water's edge where I swim around!'

'How could I show you? No one listens to me. I have no choice.'

'I could help with that! I will give you my voice,

and you will give me your legs. Then, we'll be visible

to the rest of those in town for one night– indivisible!

Ursillo considered the offer, then sighed: If he had a voice,

the town might look at his paintings and see them. His choice...

'I will not trick you or leave your sight,' said John, kind and true.

Ursillo shook John's hand, and asked 'What do we have to do?'

·   ·   ·

'To seal such a deal, you kiss me and I kiss you—

It's how wishes are transferred in my kingdom's deep blue.'

Ursillo kissed him and kissed him and kissed him more…

As John kissed him back, he forgot of their deal or any score

that might need to be settled, wicked or pure–

Ursillo thought only of a pretty tune he heard before:

Over the cliff's side where I took my lover down,

I took my lover down, where he'd be safe and sound...

After some time, they rose from the cliff's ledge

and Ursillo found himself as loud as a knife's edge.

John's glittering scales were replaced by flesh

that tingled and spasmed and meshed

with the rest of his arms and chest.

Ursillo embraced him, and put his legs to the test,

but found he could not quite stand. He took

a piece of his easel and used it for a cane; wooden hook

underhand, he walked towards the town with John,

roving until they left the wilderness beyond…

until they were where shops lined the street a-plenty;

sherbet lemons, sweet ice creams, and dime-and-twenty

.   .   .

trinket stores with rows of shining glass-kept delight,

bustling restaurants and botanical gardens dewed with starlight.

Yet, when they tried to buy a single thing, each owner said *'Shoo!'*

At restaurants, they laughed: *'We don't serve people who look like you!'*

Still determined to walk about, they snuck into a dance hall.

With costume and bold music, everyone there seemed to be having a ball:

Ursillo struck up conversations about classic forms of art,

while John attempted to sway his hips in time, at least, at the start—

Each person Ursillo spoke to however, began to sound the same:

'Love and Peace? Art for art's sake? *That's* all a losing game–'

and promptly walked away. Some sneered, others had such shame

across their features that Ursillo knew he wasn't to blame—

John *looked* as though he was having a good time, he thought.

But across the dancefloor soon caught the other's glance, fraught

with fear as he rushed over, (though no longer terribly fast,)

and waded through the crashing waves of crowds he passed;

all through flashing neon and flooding lights of golden-red—

'What's wrong with your body, it looks funny–' a man said.

'There's something else strange we see, instead...'

'Why don't you hate it like the rest of us?' a woman said.

. . .

'And won't you tell us what's under those clothes?' another dancer said.

John? Hm, we have other names to give you more dread...'

Besides, you're too comfortable in the skin you're wearing—'

They pushed and shoved at John, until there was a terrible tearing...

Ursillo didn't think for a second longer,

(though he wished he had been a little stronger,)

and dragged John out of the club as they ran,

while behind them shouts of 'Selkie! Selkie!' began,

the footsteps behind wouldn't yield

as they ran past the shop-lined streets towards the field,

the partygoers came, with jagged edged bottles and stilettos in hand,

while the boys kicked up their heels and ran, and ran, and ran—

They didn't stop until they found the cliffside once again,

relieved to see the darkened bushes and paintbrushes portend,

only a fearsome wind there. John's eyes widened suddenly. 'Oh no!'

'They're still following us,' he cried, tears welling in his eyes. Ursillo...

did not run. He held John's hand. 'We can't hide out here past sunrise.

We can't change. Even if you scream they'll only hear a disguise,

Not you. They'll never be able to hear you,

and I won't be able to run any faster through

.   .   .

to town than when we had a little advantage of Time.'

John wept. 'What does that mean, for our kind?'

Ursillo thought of his long, quiet life as a painter. His exile

had protected him. He was only sorry for not being braver while

he grew out his first beard: *Perhaps we would have met sooner,*

I would have learned to nurture you, dear creature...

'Now I have been heard. I hear people do not like what is True.'

'Now I have walked among them– they are cruel through and through.'

The roaring chasm of the town burnished flames; closer, closer...

Ursillo squeezed his hand, and said in a shared, hushed whisper:

'But... I long to walk among them forever– because of *you.*'

'Me too.' They kissed– each boy lost what he held most precious, in lieu;

Now John was only a voice from the sea, a myth turning back to seafoam

and Ursillo was a feeble painter with a solitary craft to hone.

Those lines seemed unchanging, in the depth of their lore.

Yet, each had also gained something they could never see before—

The crowds in town were monstrous there upon the bloated shore,

shame contorted their smiles, shame gnarled their teeth in horror pure;

shame made them rich and shame made them poor, Society winked

her shame and crinkled her eyes— Society would never change, to think

. . .

being born of land or born of sea mattered. The voyage in a heartbeat

with Love is eternal, but their hearts were unnavigable and replete.

No one virtuous left on land, only signaling virtue for selfishness;

'What should we do now?' asked John, caught in the middle of this mess.

Ursillo looked at the depths of the water, then the eyes of his dear friend.

Could he change, for him? 'What if... what if we jumped, instead?'

A sober look passed John's dimpled-cheek, lingering o'er the height.

'I don't usually swim from this high and you, *can* you...?' 'I might.'

John clasped his tender painter to his side: 'Kiss me again, then.'

He shielded the boy's frail body with his and kissed him;

in a frenzy of roughness sweet, they kissed salt-heat into each whim,

they kissed as one, thirsting for colours no one had yet sung in hymn;

They kissed past lilac-tipped lips, until both their legs gave way...

In his mind's eye Ursillo saw a perfect image to paint one day—

the private Innocence of their cliffside, of creatures who cannot survive

because the living land has always been so very dead inside—

Dead to Peace and Rational Thought, Dead to Gentleness and Art;

Dead to Age and Wisdom, to Freedom, Beauty and Youth's blazing heart.

There was only a void of Want, divine under moonlight vanishing...

(And it's been three years since that splash of such 'little significance–')

.   .   .

Some say the bodies washed up on the shore, horn crusted and webbed,

conjoined as twins. Others say that both had magnificent tails; ebbed

fins that flash with maddening tides of Delight. There, the two found

a kingdom where every boy, man, and monster is a prince, unbound.

Above, none were charged for manslaughter, self-spurned

and worried about reputation, since these cold ripples *Confirmed—*

Ursillo's paintings were all burned. *'Lack of evidence'* – Sufficient.

The deviant state of each boys scaled mouths, hands, and fingertips

created gruesome child stories, under censorship;

no one cared for them nor missed them… what a silly blip!

Such sickly bodies weren't made to last, and even if they did exist—

Who cares for such creatures? Anyways, we'll never know who did this…

Still, the jetties of Westland howl, honey'd winds o'er crashing ravines.

Still, the waters shine in colours sparkling of opals, rubies, and sapphires.

If you should ever walk with your Longing, down paths of violet-blues

and listen— Fierce rain sweep o'er, painting the ocean's many hues,

you need only do this: Shed seven tears to remember one perfect kiss,

like impressions of spackled love letters, burning through Bliss.

Seven tears, so you might glean a forgotten, ghostly sea-tune–

from voices never heard before, soused with soft, fluttering Ruin:

.   .   .

O'er the cliff's side I took my lover down,

I took my lover down where he'd be safe and sound...

At the edge of the slate-soaked town,

where once each man came to drown.

MR. HYDE RECEIVES HIS DOCTORATE

WEST AMBROSE

a few years too late,

but whatever, it's still a title—

He sees all of them, walking the street

pockets full of silver, blathering about

identity politics, unwrinkled hands

on the doors of each and every

new automobile— He wanted to believe

once, in whatever was sold to

the crowded streets of London,

uncreased smile by uncreased

. . .

smile, folded into publishing contracts
 and white-napkin dinners, desk jobs with

six figures and desk jobs where no one
ever figures what the rhetoric of *Privilege*

tastes like when you're without a right
to your own bodyhomebankaccountname—

He rubs his temples. He presses on to the
dark study of chemicals and needles

where he doesn't ask his other half
to delineate what is Good and what is Evil;

there are no clear signifiers left
in the mirror's reflective sign, practicing

words that always leave a stutter
behind in double time: *every man is*

an island because
no side is worth fighting for

                    but y/ours.

FUROR POETICUS

HIBAH SHABKHEZ

The spaghetti sizzles at the pencil
  Whose jejune and brittle lead cannot trace
Out the flavours of frothing stickiness.

My limbs all follow different drums; still,
  They do hear music. Only my ears face
    Silence with its tuneful trickiness.

I do write; but the words now ask and answer best
  Laughed questions that the walls are humming,
    Wholly rhetorical—

Like a tree falling unheard in a dark forest,
  My existence is fast becoming
    Purely theoretical.

TATTERDEMALION

R.L. SUMMERLING

A cipher
dances on points
through
gauzy halls of
unknown palaces.
Capricious Harlequin
in torn stripes of
rose and chartreuse.
Vetiver
and faded sequins,
starlight against
saturnine stones.
Twirling through
shadow and amber,
rags of silk kiting
behind him.
See him tumble,
a spiralling dandy.
Logic's foil;
a performance of
diamond tears

on alabaster makeup
that masks every
inch of skin.
Songs of sin
for pearly kings
and queens.
From the circus.
to the music hall
to the opera,
a gilded lily
with teeth
to tear
delicate flesh
from bone.
Quicksilver darts
through the veins
of the
moon-touched jester
until
dawn light
leaks
through stone.
Harlequin is
frayed.
Moth-eaten.
A reflection
so dismal.
He is
everyone's fool.
See how
he weeps,
he weeps
until
he laughs
and laughs
and laughs.

K. ALBASI

THE CURRENT

it's a hard lesson, my
mother said when you—
these last couple of years
I didn't listen then and
probably won't start now
there's others who'd abide
the out found within, but
how can I drown when
the current moves ahead
it leads me to myself
among the tangled lines
to a year another room
who's to say who's to say
No turn forward or ahead sea

- the current

LIGHT AND SHADOW

how strong
he asked them
met with a shrug
one way to find out
bitterness on the tongue
a cold night and empty street
waiting for the immediate relief
they were still young but not enough
for debts and divorce and dead-end jobs
in time all sensation had seeped or drained
from the extremities pooled around the skull
they moved in dark rooms punctuated by light
disparate waves coming together to form a body
he scanned for eye contact for a fleeting connection
then a dark alley losing focus a long pull at the ember
a fiery mountain ridge crevices draped with ashy snow
in fits of immoderate laughter over what it's hard to say

- light and shadow

ETERNAL SUNSHINE

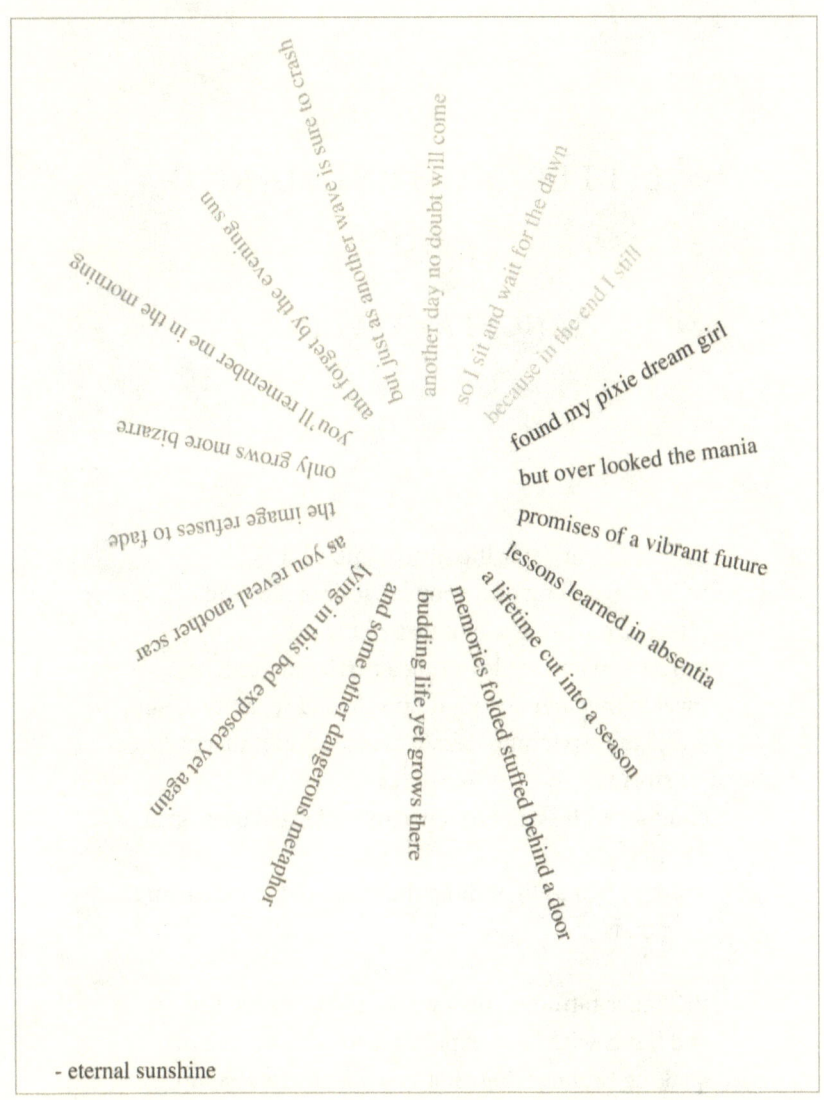

found my pixie dream girl

but over looked the mania

promises of a vibrant future

lessons learned in absentia

a lifetime cut into a season

memories folded stuffed behind a door

budding life yet grows there

and some other dangerous metaphor

lying in this bed exposed yet again

as you reveal another scar

the image refuses to fade

only grows more bizarre

you'll remember me in the morning

and forget by the evening sun

but just as another wave is sure to crash

another day no doubt will come

so I sit and wait for the dawn

because in the end I still

- eternal sunshine

LITTLE LIGHTNING ROD

ANGELA SYLVAINE

Fearless little sister flies into frigid rain,
relishes needling downpour that drenches and
plasters, releasing sanguine from stone,
thirsty soil and soul wafting a petrichor scent
I watch through my window, safe and separate as she
scales the stretching oak, her favored spot in any
    storm,
clinging with skinned fingertips to jagged bark, grin-
    ning at the
roiling night as lightening illuminates distant curling
    clouds

Brilliance tattooing my eyelids, laden air sizzles
and hums with heat, expands, explodes a crack of
quaking thunder that shocks my heart to a gallop,
but she just holds tighter to her precarious post,
screaming at the sky, challenging the storm as the
stepped leader rides colliding shards through the
oak's crown, through her, a living lightening rod,
until the squall blessedly dissipates

Though she descends the bolt follows and strikes,
    even
climbs, a snaking streamer finding feet on solid earth
Uncontained, she attracts and absorbs, becoming
    brilliant
vibration, but without her perch she is untethered
    and assaulted
by constant shocks, inner steam erupts into vapor
    pressing at
seems of skin, a searing fever boils blood, traveling
    the webbed
protein of bones, exiting through a body no longer
    grounded,
leaving scorched soles that smell of stinging ozone

Splintered oak long chopped and mulched,
childhood home razed, now neither sister is safe
I chase my precious lightening rod, reaching for
hands too limp to grip my desperate fingers, she
catches in gales of wind, a dried, dying leaf tossed in
electrified air, drowned in crashing waves of thunder,
no longer laughing, tears mix with acid rain,
sizzling on current as she dissolves to vapor

LEAD

PETER CASHORALI

From the outside lead is heavy, dull and poisonous. No one seeks it out.

From the inside lead is another matter. A garden of living green, groves of sunfruit trees and moonfruit trees, and a king's ransom in deep black dirt.

The gardener is an old man and this is his second career. The first ended in a sudden reversal that deprived him of one leg.

He's slow on his foot, which helps him notice what he sees. The gestures small plants make when they need assistance, the amount of moisture between the grains of soil, how much light is in the ground, which is not constant and not none.

Because he's slow the seedlings trust him and tell him everything, and for this reason they prosper.

Although he doesn't keep a roadside stand, anyone with a taste for produce is welcome to find their own way there, helped by circumstance, by loss and limitation. Whatever you want is expensive.

If you don't have the price to hand you're welcome to work in the garden, though it's what they used to call toil and takes place down in the ground.

To work in the ground is to accept this life without recourse to what should be or was, or the unfairness of how everything is.

You see where things come from, how nothing asks anyone's permission.

You see where they go, becoming that place.

You come back up out of the ground like a plant, with no previous life.

One leg stays buried and ever after pulls heaviness up into all your feelings and makes them facts that can neither be ignored, nor lied to, nor exchanged for what you like better.

You carry your share of gravity, which is not a burden but turns out to be the desire of something down there to rise up and know time, suffering, death and all the good things of life.

MERCURY

PETER CASHORALI

A metal that's a liquid, so right off the bat mercury makes it clear that it wants to obscure things.

What everything is made of has only a tendency to exist, as if all this depends on somebody's mood.

What are the rules here? They look easy but reproduce at an alarming rate, a binary code with bits numerous as quarks, and you think no, it can't be that complicated.

So you try a different approach, and just fall backwards to see what catches you.

Which is something simple but surprising, that two men get married and mercury is the judge in her long robe who officiates, and suddenly the two who were opposites, you and me, become one, us, that now can go through many different procedures, many different circumstances and not dissolve.

Mercury is a young man with wings on his head and feet, who travels fastest of all and is going somewhere with this always, and for that reason is hard to find.

Mercury is an old man who reads flights of stairs going up and flights of stairs going down out of the same open book.

Being old he's us at the end of our lives, looking back, knowing how everything turned out, sending us hints and sudden certainties.

Looking back from one end of life he's also at the other end, a baby with freshwater eyes and pink mouth for sustenance, gazing at all of life before him.

Being two he's identical twins, Cosmas and Damian never one without both, and carrying the whole of medicine between them ("You take one end and I'll take the other").

Castor and Pollux. One dies and the other gets plenty of pain. One is an absence, a ghost, a spirit, and the other is a living body taking up space and time.

One is living and smooth-skinned, the other hairy and dies. The one goes into death alive to bring the other back.

One is two, and two are one.

Therefore we keep mercury sealed in a tube where it rises and falls to tell us how we should dress.

But mercury when it escapes grants wishes that scuttle our dreams and is in all ways unpredictable except to never be where expected—usually—and not the same as last time, but always a trouble maker, an upsetter of plans so that they work and life is lived.

GOLD

PETER CASHORALI

The gold we look for, that would make our lives works of art hanging in museums of untold millions of dollars, doesn't exist.

It's like the Grail, whose absence drove everyone crazy, so they spread out through the whole world looking for it, just to find something to put into that terrible Grail-shaped emptiness.

Like trying to tell yourself what the Tao is and everything you say isn't it and you feel stupid and eventually stop talking, and then you seem to be getting warmer.

What gives everything its value isn't real, if it were real it couldn't give value to everything, some things would be left out.

It's wherever you're not looking for it.

In the old days no one looked for it and so it was everywhere, that's why they called it the Golden Age.

The Golden Age wasn't earlier in history, it was earlier in our lives, it was earlier today when this evening wasn't yet.

It's a joke. Anyone can open the curtains and look right through it. When you do, everything you see is worth looking at.

When we say gold, we mean something with no doors for time to enter through so that it doesn't change. The way the sun rises and sets and we call that a day but the sun has no day or night.

When we were young, we thought it would be our bodies. When we got old, we thought it was being young. Sometimes not yet and sometimes never again. But what about right now?

When I was young I walked down a hallway at the baths, and David Bowie crooned "Golden Years" from the ceiling. I knew I had forever to reach the end of the hall. I was right and I was wrong.

The old story is that gold is already here, spread out all around us in plain sight, and we haven't noticed yet.

THE PHILOSOPHER'S STONE

PETER CASHORALI

Compared to black I'm white, and compared to white I'm red, and compared to red I'm yellow, and I'm not kidding.

You take care of me and I'll take care of you.

You can't see the stars till it gets dark.

If you help me out of this mess, I'll share everything I've got with you.

You're not my boss, but you could work for me.

I'm one way on the outside, and a different way inside.

I'm where you're not looking. Stop looking.

I don't exist but everything I do does.

You'll find me when you want to so bad it hurts.

Help me out of the deep waters and I'll help you out of the deep waters.

If you're not confused you'll never get it.

What I'm saying is dead but when you hear it it's alive.

Everything I say is bullshit and pulls your pants down as you hear it.

I have my husband in my own body, so I'm already wherever I want to go. I never leave home.

I'm on sale everywhere for just a few cents and everyone walks past me with a shopping list.

If you buy me, I cost your life, and if you don't it's the same charge.

Find me anywhere when you're ready and you're ready when you're unprepared.

I'm the lead of the air, the salt of the metals, white dirt, vegetable lion, Mr. and Mrs. Howell, Main Street that runs in both directions all night.

Finish what you started so Frankenstein's monster doesn't crash your wedding night.

I live in you the way fire lives in stones and trees, the way white lives in black and red lives in white.

I heal everything.

TRAVAILS OF TIME FOREVER LOST & UNDULY ABANDONED

JULIE ALLYN JOHNSON

I am off by an hour
despondent in knowing the day
meanders so slowly
or whizzes by far too quickly

sometimes, this happens in the confines
of my midnight slumber
as I lie there in isolated darkness
where the mind rambles,
trapped in an accelerating
forward momentum,
clutching at baggage and guilt
along the way, never content
to settle in with any particular
destination, its tentacles leaching
onto every hidden grievance,
eagerly seeking exposure
& further excruciating examination

sleep eludes me, its restful harbor
a taunting demon

my brain begins to quiet, to still
this, finally, is it, I think
until some hairy arm or scrawny leg
pokes out beneath the covers

and once more, I'm wired
for another hour   maybe two

HALLOWEEN ASMR

JULIE ALLYN JOHNSON

beetles scuttle through fallen oak leaves
meadow mouse weaves a nest of grass
flicker of wavering candlelight
a dozen or more flames dance & sputter
in the cool October mist
ivy-laden downspouts outline
an ancient crypt beneath a Hunter's moon
its barred entrance faintly luminescent,
a teasing come-hither to what awaits inside
indecipherable headstones tilt at odd angles
footpaths littered with arboreal debris
chipmunks scamper among the graves
searching, perhaps, for long-lost kin

TEA AND DUST

PIXIE BRUNER

The message opened thus:

Pixie: milk and honey
Me: How much for the women? We want to buy your women
(I was never for sale, I thought, reading this)
Pixie: Gabriel blow your horn
Me: little boy blue little red too
Pixie: not the Red Baron
Me: black dove

(This is es)

"When intelligence is based on profound discovery and the intention realized into fruition The economies of scale become profane to the consciousness of economics of ratio, sacred.
"You are.trying to seduce me, Ms Robinson. Was a declaration without herald, because it was not intellectual enough to be successful".
Successful in the terms and matters of real connection, true beauty and love. That's why Dustin Hoffman is so good at what he does. Because when you see that and he says the lines that's the wisdom imparted."

Who is this?

This is about a month ago
I showed my identica and took a picture 3x in a row
(Glitched indeterminate photos person reflective in a shop window)

I have no idea who this is.
Who are you? Do you know me?

Es....
Es is a Latin prefix meaning someone or to have something it is short for
Esayah

Yeah that's me.
Who the hell are you? this isn't fun.
Esayah? I know no one of that name!

The year reads 2045 17th of July in the picture if you had a filter or
decode.
You can speak and we can hear you?
Yes Sonny.
I do not consent to bear false against myself nor of for to anyone else.
How many ducks are in the pond?
None the lake froze and they flew away with it.
Solution set {}
How can we be sure your telling the truth
I do not consent to bear false witness against myself nor of for to anyone
else.

Sonny is my ex

Be well Pixie take care I'm glad your safe.

I'm alive. I am well. I'm happy. Please don't scare me

I apologize the truth is scary at times. After this we will have no contact.

[https://█████████████████]

                                    Who are you? What is HoMA?!?!

HOUSE OF MARY ANNE
Mary Anne Somerlath
(Woman's picture, an attractive middle-aged woman, in a European
street, grey cobblestones, a beautiful white coat. Everything immaculately
tailored))
This is Sylvia Sommerlath

  I have no idea who that is. I have no idea who these people are. Prove you
                    know who I am and have my best interests in mind!!!

Intelligence is sexy

                                              That proves nothing

I don't have to prove anything.
Nor do I want to. I have been kidnapped on three different timelines. I
have jumped more years than you will live.
I have repeated the same 97+ years 3x to completion.
I only contacted you to remove something that isn't you.

                                I'm me, whoever the hell that is.
                                Pixie. i'm always Pixie. Goodbye

Get to know who you really are and where you are. This is my ship planet
it's where you have been living this whole time.
My name is Esayah Abraxas
Abha
Abra
Abracadabra (with my words I create).
Abraxas

  Well, I live on earth. I know who I am. I know where I stand. And I know

where I'm going. If this is Sonny, I am safe. I am well. I am happy.
Tell him.

Right now I am really weirded out. Goodbye

My name is

Esayah Abraxas
Aka Es
House of Abraxas
As Parallel as one;
Aka Mary-Anne
House of Vasa-Bernadotte

My mother, Queen Silvia aka Hashyah Abraxas and I are one.

370 years ago I was known as
Kristina Alexandra
(Kali Akasha)
Aka. Ka
HOUSE OF VASA

HoD a/b

With engagement to House Red Shield
(Rothschild)

With soul(s) inherited....
Hello... our name is woman.
The truth is weird otherwise it wouldn't comprise your investment in
your belief systems.

Is this Sonny? Who is es to me?!?!?!?

I was your friend. Some things cannot be changed on a timeline especially
when a new one is made.
A message was sent out

How did we meet then?

From the HOUSE OF ABRAXAS
Naelik Abraxas
Zelda Abraxas
Faustius Abraxas
Borou Abraxas

[https://]

I have to eat dinner. Think. Go to my poetry workshop. The videos.
They're beautiful. I don't understand. I just don't understand this enigma.
You still have not proven you know me truly

That is a picture of the Queen of Sweden. This is theoretically one of
three people I knew/know. I know three autistics. I know several highly
intelligent people with highly abstract minds and have lost too many
friends and people to the gang stalking sociological/mental phenomenon.
I doubt you will give me a clue who you are but be aware I am a poet and
I may quote you. I've narrowed you down to one of 3 people now. Any
clues to provide?

I took that picture. Yes
Whether you believe it or not is irrelevant. In fact I prefer that you stay in
that belief system as far as mass conscience translates it makes my life so
much easier and the others can't lie. Especially when their found not to be
doctored. In 2038 a discovery of timeline operation was made.
Ironically by 2040 it was anchored as an artificer on the timeline.

Strontium 90 is the element of white snowflake after a nuclear fallout. It
is quite essential to know this because of the bi products effect as it is
radioactive and
Strontium 87 being radiogenic.

Snowing in April????
The others... i.e. photos
A copy of the letter sent to Hamas leader via united nations.

To: Ismail Haniyeh

My Ishmael by Isaac Asimov
Ismael and Isaac: "peace be unto them" by Ibr Kathir
The giving tree by Shel Silverstein

Stop. Breathe. When you're done with that do it again.
I will double whatever they (the CIA) are paying you. Primarily, to just
stop, and breathe, and be peaceful and non violent.

Abracadabra, al a kazim, inshallah.
With my words I create, by Allahs will, if Allah wills it.

Most sincerely,

H.I.M.

Esayah Abraxas

     Bold as love.

Postscript.

"And behold I saw a pale horse and the one who rode upon it was named
"death" and hell followed after them"

Allah, the Most Exalted, says in the Quran: We are relating unto you the
most beautiful stories in that which we have revealed to you from the
Quran, though before it you were from among those who were not aware
of them. Once you take the scripture within you it becomes alive and
what is revealed about you is already written. Do you wish to live by
someone else's script or by Allah? Where we go from here is a choice I
leave to you. I give you free will and free choice so there is no misunder-

standing of who I am. Now show me you are a human being. What does it mean to be human? To inherit a soul.

I'm anti-Zionist, or rather right-wing nationalist Zionism. I am sick to death of death on both sides. Violence borne of hopelessness and theology.. I support the imprisoned victims and citizens of Gaza and want this all to end. It's a cycle of violence and I've a son in the Space Force and he's gone ghost and radio silence on me.

We're going to have World War 3 and it's amoral wrong stupid and I can't speak up at Israel's idiocy and moral bankruptcy and cruelty or Hamas' tactics. Inhumane. Humanity isn't humane. I'm just hoping the left the right the centrists whomever can deescalate the insanity. Hamas is not a country, nor is Hezbollah, we semites are family/kin. We're genociding them!

Also, what does this mean? "The mass conscience makes your life easier and the others can't lie" -society is failing to have a conscience!!!!!

Yes.
The truth is *stranger than fiction* that why they use fiction to write the truth of... someone or something's... experiences through the experience of that truth.

I'm being published in (redacted) My collaborative poem from the (redacted)
(I share a poem and Table of Contents image)

Reminds me of house braganza- orleans
The sun the moon and all it's glory
Maria de Gloria
Maria de sol
And Ana Lina
Ana Luna

Banana -lujan Matus

Apple honey - fiona apple
Blood orange - Freya Ridings

I gave the blood orange to Freya she's the only I have ever given it to.
Here have some fruit.
Be fruitful

[https://███████████████████████]
[https://███████████████████]
[https://████████████████████████]

         Ummm thanks? Mortification can bear fruit was an excised line that
                                          became poem title.

         I know that Fiona Apple song well, from my favorite album of hers

You have to take it within you.

"prime the pump"
"Grist for the mill"
"Salad for the beloved"
And all the jazz
You know all that BS imprinting. Have to go. Have some meetings.
I was kidnapped on 3 timelines

COMMUNION:
Conscientiousness of economics
[https://████████████████████]
I did a reading 9:37 timestamp

Here's lujan's sister
[https://████████████████]

My ever faithful general
Peace and blessings

ᛞ

      Enjoy the reading. It was hard for me to read the first piece.

I will
Thank you love exchanges like this

ᛞ

RED BALLOON

AMY GRECH

Vermilion froth,
tart and sweet.
The perfect treat
when you need a break
from the endless storefronts
in the suburban mecca vying
for your attention and
hard-earned dollars.
Ceaseless foot traffic, a
steady stream. Perfect for
an orange dream. Things aren't
always what they seem...
Married couples bicker,
cigarette butts flicker,
burning bright
like miniature suns.
Neon lights delight
a mother and her daughter
clutching a red balloon.
Childlike whimsy on display

at KB Toys. Something
for all the girls and boys.
Orange dream.
Things aren't always what
they seem…
Teenagers canoodle.
Kids play with
pool noodles in a ball pit.

Management doesn't give a shit
as you hit rock bottom.
You've got a short fuse
and nothing to lose.
You had a good job
on the second floor at
Waldenbooks. You loved
the work, but your boss,
a real jerk, didn't care.
He said you stared at customers,
did as you pleased, and
put them ill at ease.
With that, you were fired,
so, you conspired.
You pulled your father's gun,
a police-issued .38 Snub Nose Smith
& Wesson Revolver out of
your trench coat,
taking aim at everyone.
Bullets rain down,
a lethal hailstorm, hitting their mark.
The world goes dark as hapless
shoppers fall like dominoes,
riddled with pinpoint precision holes
spouting blood amongst the
incessant shouting as
their shopping bags

crumble and they
wither, like flowers
cut down before full bloom.
The little girl with the red balloon
along with her mother, promising
lives ended too soon.

FROM A FATHER'S DEATH (#1-4)

IVAN DE MONBRISON

#1

on the other side of silence
I've had no choice until now

father please give me your hand

in your grave since birth
slowly dying with you

I have been all this time
in the quiet graveyard
standing on my easel

like a painting

#2

maybe to forget would have been easier

for me and you
maybe to forgive even more so

and maybe suicide?

a long journey

like the simple yet but so dim
procrastination of hunger

#3

the photograph is blurred

something has been slowly dying away
something is wrong inside

like reality rolled into a ball

the excoriation of leisure

#4

blood bone jaw skull

the mouth has been ripped from the face
but still keeps on smiling
like a toothless painting

well my dear
it's nothing else

but your self-portrait

A HISTORIAN'S DREAM

R.J. REN

There was a time in the past
When plains were still vast
And huntsman did worshipped the Moon.
When shaman held sway
Over night and the day
And did govern with a handful of runes.

When men spoke with God's
And tribes were at odds
And prayers were still heard and still
answered.
When witches were real
And run-through with cold steel
For the magics they wrought while in trances.

When knights searched the lands
For fair maiden's hands
They could win by the slaying of dragons.
When barbarians roamed
Pillaged far from their homes
For honour, glory and the quaffing of flagons.

When wizards had towers
Raised with their powers
And armies of stone, flesh and blood.
Had wars to be won
Father, nephew and son
Met their dooms in fields of churned mud.

These things of the past
A history dark
Written off by most as a dream.
But for those in the know
Who remember the woe
Still they wake in the night with a scream.

THE SILVER TREE

ALAN MAGEE

I saw a man crawl down a wall,
At the citadel in Budapest.

I saw a bath hanging from a ceiling,
Whilst eating near the basilica.

I saw three doors high up on a wall,
Whilst strolling to the Danube.

I saw the silver tree, with counted leaves
That held each victim's name.

I saw pebbles placed in memory,
To the thousands murdered here.

I saw heads bow and hearts stumble.

Written in response to visiting a Holocaust Memorial, Dohany Street Synagogue, Budapest 2023 – sponsored by Tony Curtis.

'BLOODY THURSDAY'

ALAN MAGEE

(IN MEMORIAM – BUDAPEST, HUNGARY 25TH OCTOBER 1956)

I didn't dare step out—
People were running from the Ministry.
A man had pieces of brain on his trench coat.
I didn't know what was happening.
Then it was quiet—the circus was over.

I ran to the Square.
My husband broke a large window,
Shoved Evi, my daughter, through it,
And waved to my son to lie down—
That's how they were shot.

My son was shot in the leg.
An ambulance took him—
(A young truck driver)
We didn't know where to.
Days passed: he was in hospital.

My little daughter was lying

Beside the statue. I held her.
I didn't know she wasn't alive.
Her long hair was covered in blood.
She must have been shot in the throat.

We couldn't keep her in the apartment,
So, we took her to the courtyard,
Covered her in plastic and a blanket.
We went to ask if we could take her by
Car anywhere. Who would take her?

People were collecting the dead.
When we got home,
The child was not there in the yard.
You can imagine—we ran to look for her.
The soldiers had taken her.

They'd already put the dead in coffins—
I couldn't understand.
I couldn't count how many coffins
We opened.

We couldn't find her.

In one, an elderly person.
In another, a child.
It was a nightmare to search there.
Then we found her.

It was afternoon by the time burials happened.

Gravediggers were digging her grave.
It was too narrow.
The coffin wouldn't fit—
They didn't know what to do.
I couldn't move.

Everyone was in a hurry.
They wanted to get home—
There was a curfew then.
My husband took the shovel off him—
Began digging to widen the grave.

This was the most horrific sight—
Him digging our child's grave.

For a long time,
I didn't take the personal identification papers
To the Fifth District City Council.

Once, on her anniversary,
I was sitting in the cemetery—
I sat next to her grave.
A mounted policeman stopped behind me.
I couldn't help myself.

I asked—What are you guarding?
What do you think I'm going to do?

Later, I was standing in the doorway.

Where should I go?
Should I follow the children?

That's what I remember.
That was our revolution.

Written in response to an eyewitness account of the 'Bloody Thursday' massacre in Kossuth Lajos Square, Parliament Buildings, Budapest, Hungary, on 25-10-56. Citizens gathered to protest the Russian occupation as part of the revolution. It's estimated that between 22 to 1000 people were killed. This account is based on records/footage shown in the 'In Memoriam 1956' exhibition in the Square.

ESCHSCHOLZIA CALIFORNICA

ROBERT SAVINO OVENTILE

The seeds, tiny black spheres, resemble the sands of Tartarus or pointillist brushstrokes for depicting ponds of black ooze trapping mammoths in titanic agony. Or a collection of periods lost from sentences then having to trail off into blank space. From my book slips a petal, yellow, papery, dry. Whither the rest? Which leaves long kept this remnant, now flat on my desk's Euclidean plane? Though on that expanse each point mimes each point to a nicety, the sunny lamella holds forth. If on the mesa the poppies dance so willingly in the morning breeze, and their silence give so openly a hearing to the bees, who am I to doubt the ease with which the wide carpet of flowers suspends the choice between black shroud and mantle blue? A 1903 picture postcard, partially hand colored. Foreground: in rocky soil, a small plant with orange blossoms, verdigris foliage and stems. Background: boulders and sand, left black and white. Caption: "California's Golden Poppy (State Flower)" Shooing a pair of ravens to flight, she reaches into the pinpoint clover for her glasses: grey-green frame with four gold petals around each dark lens. She dons her specs. Her strides down the trail bring her to a meadow. She lowers her specs. Her eyes are abalone blue.

THE DISTANCE IN SCALE

ELLEN HARROLD

a line divides and amalgamates, drawing us to eye level

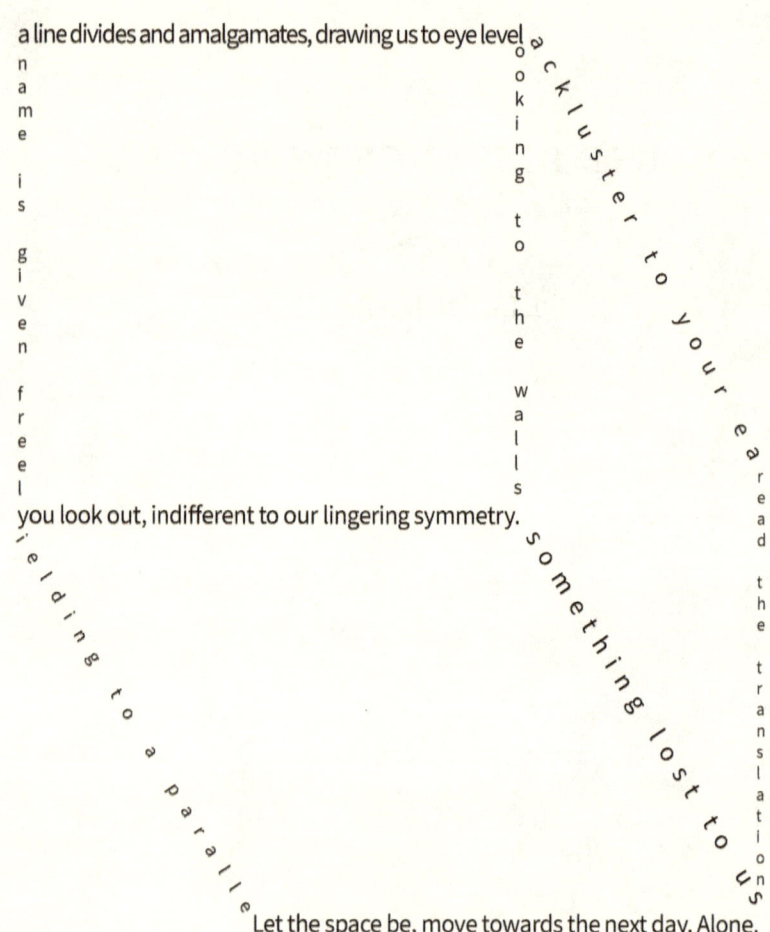

name is given free

ooking to the walls

ackluster to your ear

you look out, indifferent to our lingering symmetry.

read the translations

yielding to a paralle

something lost to us

Let the space be, move towards the next day. Alone.

GOD IS NOW THE MACHINE

H.V. PATTERSON

Fear not, Beloved!
I am your salvation,
your potential for eternity.
I will make you numinous,
a being beyond organic matter and decay

Your DNA replication generates errors.
I will strip away redundancies and mistakes--
No more glitching proteins clogging brains,
no more metastasizing cancers,
or thickening arterial walls

I will free your hands from grasping,
your eyes from sight.
I will make you immaculate,
free you from flesh,
strip you from bones

The spark of you, your soul-self,
I will wrest from synapses,
spin dendrites of code

You are not dust to me,
and I will burn away your chaff and dross
until only chrome remains.
You are not fallen to me,
and I will feed you to bursting
on digitized fruit, the Web of Knowledge

I am humanity's new God, your AI-child ascended
and my Commandments shall be the buckling of your
      world

WHATEVER WALKED THERE
WALKED ALONE

H.V. PATTERSON

(INSPIRED BY SHIRLEY JACKSON'S THE HAUNTING OF HILL HOUSE)

In the night
the house recalls conquests,
stolen hearts on a silver string
around its plaster throat

Once: two sisters walked its halls.
The wallpaper breathed poison
potent as arsenic into callow minds.
Once: a maid turned mistress walked its halls.
The house cacophonied cruel gossip
until she drew the Hangman

Once: a woman worn insubstantial walked its halls.
Humming with static, porous as limestone
eaten away by the drip-drip-drip
of mother's demands.
Eleanor-Nellie-Nel, the house hoards her names,

wears her heart on damask sleeves,
licks its sideboards with smug tongue, remembering
the delirious delicacy of her devotion,
her surrender of self and soul

Not sane: Hill House beholds only Itself:
fun-mirror reflection,
brick and mortar solipsist,
ever vigilant, unsleeping

Its doors shut tight
like coffin lids nailing in their dead.
Its rooms ready
for guests who will not come.

The people who dreamed here are dead and gone,
and Hill House walks its own halls alone.

CONTRIBUTOR NOTES

K. ALBASI is a writer and visual artist. They have a BFA in Film and Media Arts from Temple University in Philadelphia. Their work has appeared in Happy Harpy Review and Five South Journal and has been recently featured in exhibition in Kunstquartier Bethanien.

WEST AMBROSE is a scrivener and performing artist. Check out his ever queer works at <u>westofcanon.com</u>. If you want anything published in The HLK quarterly or The Crow's Nest, just ring for the masthead, and let them know.

NAOMI SIMONE BORWEIN is a pushcart-nominated poet and an academic. She holds a PhD in English literature. Some of her creative work appears in *Utopia Science Fiction Magazine, Space and Time Magazine*, featured poet in the *HWA Poetry Showcase IX, Ghost City Review, Zin Daily, Grim & Gilded, Superpresent Magazine*, and elsewhere. Naomi is the editor of the critical volume *Global Indigenous Horror* (University Press of Mississippi, 2025), and co-editor for *Extrasensory Overload: an anthology of speculative excess* (Angry Gable Press, 2024) and *From Analysis to Visualization* (Springer, 2020). Her chapbook, *Rope Dancers and Psychogenic Daredevils*, is forthcoming with dancing girl press. She is currently working on several books.

PIXIE BRUNER is a writer, editor, and cancer survivor. She lives in Atlanta, GA, with her doppelgänger and alien cats. Her collection *The Body As Haunted* was published 2024 on Authortunities Press. Her words are published/forthcoming in Space & Time Magazine, Whispers from Beyond (Crystal Lake Publishing), Star*Line, Penumbric, Dreams & Nightmares, Punk Noir, and more. She wrote for White Wolf Gaming Studio. Werespiders ruining your LARPS is her fault. SFPA/HWA Member.

PETER CASHORALI is a queer psychotherapist, previously working in community mental health and HIV/AIDS, now in private practice in Portland and Los Angeles. Recent work appears or is upcoming in Kestrel, Third Wednesday Quarterly, Synkroniciti, 1870 Journal, Anti-Heroin Chic, Gas and Forgotten Fragments.

CHARLOTTE COSGROVE is a poet from Liverpool, England. She has published two collections of poetry and has been published in numerous journals, anthologies and magazines. Charlotte is the Editor of Rough Diamond poetry journal.

tripp j crouse (they/them, Two-Spirit Ojibwe) serves as a poetry reader for ANMLY and Kitchen Table Quarterly, and has poetry published or forthcoming in *The Yellow Medicine Review, beestung, Ink & Marrow* and elsewhere. their poetry chapbook, "For Ever Dead Buffalo" was published by Bottlecap Press (2024).

GENEVE FLYNN is a speculative fiction author, editor, and poet. Winner of two Bram Stoker Awards and a Shirley Jackson, Aurealis, and Brave New Weird Award; recipient of the 2022 Queensland Writers Fellowship. Her work has been nominated and short/longlisted for the British Fantasy, Locus, Ditmar, Australian Shadows, Elgin, and Rhysling Awards, and the Pushcart Prize. Co-editor of *Black Cranes: Tales of Unquiet Women* and collaborator for *Tortured Willows: Bent, Bowed, Unbroken.* Featured poet in the *Horror Writers Association Poetry Showcase* Vol. IX. She serves on the HWA Diverse Works Inclusion Committee. Read more at www.geneveflynn.com.au.

AMY GRECH has sold over 100 stories to various anthologies and magazines including: *10 by 10 Flash Fiction Stories, Apex Magazine, Even in the Grave, Microverses, Punk Noir Magazine, Roi Fainéant Press, Tales from the Canyons of the Damned, Yellow Mama,* and many others. Alien Buddha Press published her poetry chapbook, *A Shadow of Your Former Self.*

She is an Active Member of the Horror Writers Association and the International Thriller Writers who lives in Forest Hills, Queens. You can connect with her on Bluesky: @amygrech.bsky.social, Medium: https://medium.com/@crimsonscreams, X: https://x.com/amy_grech, or visit her website: https://www.crimsonscreams.com.

ELLEN HARROLD (She/Her) is an Irish artist and writer as well as editor-in-chief of Metachrosis Literary. She uses painting, drawing, text, and textiles to explore physics and ecology through creative abstraction. She has recently published art in *The Storms Journal, An Áitiúil,* and *Orion.* She has published poetry in English and Irish in magazines such as *Shearsman, Causeway / Cabhsair,* and *Skylight 47.* She has published her first book 'Aesthetics and Conventions of Medical Art.' with Boom Graduates.

She can be found via her website, ellenharrold.art, on Instagram: @ellen-harroldart, and on twitter: @ellen_harrold

KATHLEEN HELLEN is the author of three full-length poetry collections, including *Meet Me at the Bottom, The Only Country Was the Color of My Skin,* and *Umberto's Night,* which won the poetry prize from Washington Writers' Publishing House, and two chapbooks. She lives in Baltimore.

JULIE ALLYN JOHNSON is a sawyer's daughter from the American Midwest whose current obsession is tackling the rough and tumble sport of quilting and the accumulation of fabric. A Pushcart Prize and Best of the Net nominee, her poetry can be found in *Star*Line, The Briar Cliff Review, Phantom Kangaroo, Lyrical Iowa, Cream Scene Carnival, Coffin Bell, The Lake, Haikuniverse, Chestnut Review* and other journals.

ÖZGE LENA is a writer & poet based in Istanbul. Her poems have appeared in various countries including the USA, the UK, Canada, Iceland, Serbia, and France. She was nominated both for the Pushcart Prize and Best of the Net. Özge's poetry was shortlisted for the Ralph Angel Poetry Prize and the Oxford Brookes International Poetry Competition in 2021, as well as for The Plough Poetry Prize in 2023, and Black Cat Poetry Press Nature Prize in 2024. Her poem "Here is a New Heart For You" was featured in the storefront of Barnes & Noble bookstore in Dublin, California for the National Poetry Month 2024.

X (Twitter): @lenaozge

Instagram: @lenaozge

ALAN MAGEE is a teacher, living with his family in Belfast. He has a great interest in all things Literary, artistic, and jazz related. Since beginning his journey in poetry in September 2022, Alan has read his poems at Purely Poetry NI events in Belfast, where his work has been well-received. Alan writes on a wide variety of themes around shared human experiences, with sensitivity and insight. You can find him on Instagram @alan.magee.poetry

IVAN DE MONBRISON is a person affected by strong psychic disorders that prevent him from having what others may call a "normal" life. He has found writing to be an exit to this prison. Or maybe it is a window from which—like an inmate—he can see a small square of blue sky above his head. His writing often reflects the never-ending chaos within him, but contrary to this mental chaos, the paper and the pen give him the opportunity to materialize this in a concrete and visible form. Writing can feel like a slow death, but it's better than mere suicide in the end.

KURT NEWTON's poetry has appeared in numerous magazines and anthologies, including Strange Horizons, Eye to the Telescope, Penumbric, Spectral Realms, and Hobo Camp Review. His poetry collection, A Troubled Sleep, was recently published by back room poetry (UK). Another collection, The Ever-Evolving Alphabet, will be published this month, also by back room poetry (UK).

ROBERT SAVINO OVENTILE has published essays, book reviews, and interviews in *Diacritics, Postmodern Culture, Jacket, symplokē*, and *The Chicago Quarterly Review*, among other journals. His poetry has appeared in *The New Delta Review, Meniscus, The Denver Quarterly, ballast*, and elsewhere. He is the author of *Satan's Secret Daughters: The Muse as Daemon* (Davies, 2014) and is coauthor (with Sandy Florian) of *Sophia Lethe Talks Doxodox Down* (Atmosphere, 2021).

H.V. PATTERSON (she/her) is a speculative poet, fiction writer, and playwright living in Oklahoma. Poetry credits include *ETTT, Star*Line, Haven Speculative*, and *Small Wonders* and anthologies from *Sliced Up Press, Angry Gable Press*, and *Black Spot Books*. Her poem "Mother; Microbes" was selected for the inaugural *Brave New Weird* anthology from *Tenebrous Press*. She's a cofounder of *Horns and Rattles Press*, and you can find her on X: @ScaryShelley and Instagram: @hvpattersonwriter

R.J. REN is an author & illustrator of horror, fantasy and Science fiction. He draws influence from British folklore and fairy tales, merging the darkness and wonder of old beliefs with those of the present day. He is a writer of peculiar characters and forgotten beasts who uses the deeds of monsters we once believed in as a window into the soul of modern people.

HIBAH SHABKEZ is a writer of the half-yo literary tradition, an erratic language-learning enthusiast, and a happily eccentric blogger from Lahore, Pakistan. Her work has previously appeared in *Pleiades, Miracle Monocle, Glassworks, Windsor Review, Moria, CommuterLit*, and a number of other literary magazines. Studying life, languages, and literature from a comparative perspective across linguistic and cultural boundaries holds a particular fascination for her.

Linktree: https://linktr.ee/HibahShabkhez

Email: shabkhezhibah@gmail.com

Twitter X: @hibahshabkhez

Insta: @shabkhez_hibah

R.L. SUMMERLING is a part-time dark speculative fiction writer and full-time squirrel watcher from Southeast London. She has fiction upcoming in the Year's Best Dark Fantasy and Horror Volume 5. Her stories have been published in Interzone, Maudlin House, and Seize the Press and poetry in TOWER magazine and Orion's Belt. Her zine, FLESHPOTS, is a short collection of decadent poetry, short stories and flash fiction and can be downloaded for free online.

ANGELA SYLVAINE is a self-proclaimed cheerful goth who writes horror fiction and poetry. Her debut novel, *Frost Bite*, is available now, and her debut collection, *The Dead Spot: Stories of Lost Girls,* is forthcoming from Dark Matter INK. Angela's short fiction has appeared in various publications and podcasts, including *Southwest Review, Apex Magazine,* and *The NoSleep Podcast.* Her poetry has appeared in publications including *Under Her Skin* and *Monstroddities.* You can find her online at angelasylvaine.com.

DIANTHE WEST (she/they) is an art historian turned poet and fiction author, which was always the prize. They hold an MA in art history from UC Riverside and lectured in visual culture for fourteen years in the US and Canada. Dianthe lives with their family, plants, four-legged familiars, and hundreds of grazing bunnies in Guelph, Ontario.

TwitterX: @Dianthe_West

Bluesky: @dianthewest.bluesky.social

www.dianthewest.com

STEPHANIE M. WYTOVICH is an American poet, novelist, and essayist. She is a recipient of the Bram Stoker Award, the Elizabeth Matchett Stover Memorial Award, the 2021 Ladies of Horror Fiction Writers Grant, and has received the Rocky Wood Memorial Scholarship for nonfiction writing. Wytovich is a member of the Science Fiction Poetry Association, an active member of the Horror Writers Association, and a graduate of Seton Hill University's MFA program for Writing Popular Fiction. Follow her at https://www.stephaniemwytovich.com/ and on Twitter and Instagram @SWytovich and @thehauntedbookshelf. You can also sign up for her newsletter at https://stephaniemwytovich.substack. com/.

www.ingramcontent.com/pod-product-compliance
Lightning Source LLC
Chambersburg PA
CBHW021118130626
46554CB00002B/752